The Story of Craig Winston: An Adopted Bear

Written By: Susanne Breckwoldt, Ph.D.

Illustrated By: Allen Donahue

Discussion Guide By: Samuel Feinberg, Ph.D.

AuthorHouse™
1663 Liberty Drive
Bloomington, IN 47403
www.authorhouse.com
Phone: 1-800-839-8640

First published by AuthorHouse 7/9/2009

ISBN: 978-1-4389-9636-3 (sc)

Printed in the United States of America
Bloomington, Indiana

This book is printed on acid-free paper.

authorHOUSE®

Dedicated to my mother

C.B.

and to my friend

J.C.

With gratitude and love.
You will live on in my heart forever.

and to Buddy,

who provided
the inspiration for this book.

INTRODUCTION

To the parents, educators, school psychologists, librarians and counselors:

The story of Craig Winston, an adopted bear, is a work of fiction for children in grade levels K through 3 and their adult co-readers.

The book tells the tale of a green first-grade bear, Craig, who accidentally discovers that he has been adopted and the emotional journey he embarks on in his quest for answers.

The tale ends with Craig sitting on his mother's lap, his father sitting close by, in the confines of their cozy, safe home. The parents are about to begin their first heart-to-heart talk with Craig about his adoption. The ending serves as a natural jump-off point for discussion with your young reader(s). The discussion questions included at the end of the book can be used as a guideline to stimulate processing of the most pertinent points made in the book.

Officially Craig's story ends in his parents' living room but the most significant part of the story is yet to come:

Were the story to continue, Craig's parents would wish Craig to know:

- that he is loved and wanted and would always be their son;
- that they will share the details of Craig's unique adoption story with him;
- that they especially chose Craig to be a part of their family;
- that he can always come to them with questions and concerns;
- that they will always make time for talking;
- that this is just the first of many, many talks to come;
- that they would like to have another family meeting to include Craig's younger twin sisters so that they, also, can begin to learn about Craig's adoption, as age appropriate;
- that they will explain particulars about Craig's cultural/ethnic heritage and will explore together with Craig various opportunities for learning about his unique background, thus helping him to strengthen his sense of identity;
- that this exploration can become another bond that unites the family;

- that they can plan outings to museums highlighting Craig's culture, watch movies about Craig's cultural/ethnic heritage, collect pictures and artifacts, make a scrapbook, tap into community resources and organizations that celebrate Craig's heritage, or plan a trip to Craig's country or city of origin...the sky is the limit!

Of course, Craig's parents will need to address the issue of the unfortunate decision that Craig and Ben made to run away to the big city in search of Craig's birth parents. They will wish to validate Craig's feelings of confusion, shock and fear that served to motivate this course of action while setting strict limits and covering safety concerns.

Wishing you and yours a meaningful and joyous reading experience,

Susanne Breckwoldt

His

His name was Craig Winston. At least that was the name that he had been given. Although he was a solid colored green bear, his family, which included his 5-year-old twin sisters, Emily and Kate, and his parents, Mom and Pop Winston, were very colorful, patterned and striped, each unique yet the same nonetheless.

Craig loved being part of this colorful family. During the summertime there were lots of activities: vacations and weekends hiking, picnicking and camping out in the woods. At night Craig and his family would all sit around the campfire and have story time.

Sometimes Grandma and Grandpa Rich would come to visit. They lived in Texas and wore cowboy hats and would always bring fun presents for everyone in the family.

Mom bear would prepare an especially delicious meal and everyone would gather around the big dining room table exchanging tales and jokes and eating and laughing heartily.

It was close to the end of summer when Grandma and Grandpa Rich came to visit once again. Craig watched from the living room window as they unloaded their suitcases and bags from the car.

Craig was excited because he knew that some of those bags probably contained special presents for him because tomorrow was to be his birthday. He was going to turn 6! It was an especially important birthday because in a few days he was also going to start 1st grade in the big school across town.

After Grandma and Grandpa got settled in, the whole family gathered around the dining room table for a special birthday meal with birthday cake afterwards.

In honor of Craig's birthday, Grandma Rich gave Craig a backpack he could use for school. His Grandpa gave him a compass that his own Pa had given to him when Grandpa was just a small bear. Grandpa Rich told Craig that this was a very special gift and showed Craig how to use it. Grandpa then gave Craig a big hug and told him that because of this gift Craig would never be lost.

Craig's mom and dad gave Craig a Play Station. His little sisters gave Craig homemade birthday cards with funny pictures and hearts on them and a new notebook and colored pencils he could bring to school.

That night Craig was too excited to fall asleep. He tossed and turned in his bed. He could hear the grownups talking quietly in the living room. Craig tiptoed into the kitchen to get a glass of milk but stopped in his tracks when he heard his name being mentioned. He sneaked over to the living room entrance. The door was ajar. Craig hid behind the door so that he could listen more closely. To his astonishment he heard his Grandma ask his mom, "Did you tell Craig yet that you are not his real parents?"

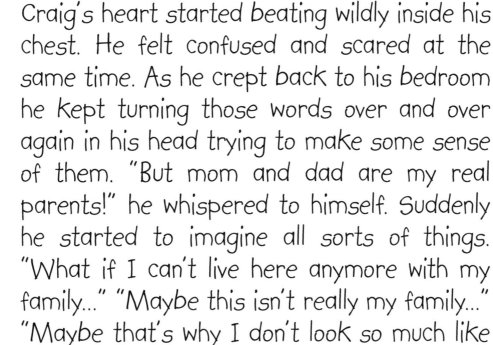
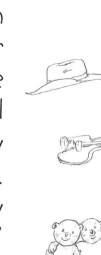

Craig's heart started beating wildly inside his chest. He felt confused and scared at the same time. As he crept back to his bedroom he kept turning those words over and over again in his head trying to make some sense of them. "But mom and dad are my real parents!" he whispered to himself. Suddenly he started to imagine all sorts of things. "What if I can't live here anymore with my family..." "Maybe this isn't really my family..." "Maybe that's why I don't look so much like my sisters and my mom and pop."

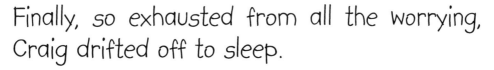

Finally, so exhausted from all the worrying, Craig drifted off to sleep.

The next few days following the birthday celebration were full of activity with Grandma and Grandpa still visiting and mom bear making lots of preparations for the start of the new school year. Craig's little sisters were also to start school. They were going to be in Kindergarten. Craig nearly forgot all about what he had overheard the other night until...

On his first day of school Craig's mom had yet another gift for him! A cell phone! Craig felt really grown up to be able to receive such a present. His mom told him that it was a very important gift and that she was giving it to him so Craig would know that he could always reach her whenever he wanted to and that she would always be able to find him no matter what. Craig's mom explained to Craig that he would not be able to use his phone during school hours but could keep the phone safely tucked away inside of his backpack.

After his mom quickly showed Craig how to use the phone, Craig stored the phone inside of his backpack and ran towards the front entrance of the elementary school along with all the other bears to begin his first day at the Crownsville Elementary School.

Craig's teacher was really nice. Her name was Ms. Page. She had glasses dangling from a pretty ribbon that she wore around her neck and a beautiful shiny pin attached to the lapels of her jacket. Ms. Page had a kind voice and warm smile for all the students.

Craig's desk was in the last row. As he scanned the other rows to see if he recognized any of his friends from the neighborhood, his heart skipped a beat when out of all of the other striped and patterned bears he saw a solid colored bear sitting in the front row.

Ms. Page asked the bears to go around the room and introduce themselves. They had to stand up and say their names and where they live. Craig discovered that the other green bear's name was Ben! He couldn't wait for recess to come around so that he could meet Ben and get to know him. He was so curious. This was the first time Craig had ever seen another solid colored bear close up.

At recess Ms. Page took Craig's class outside to the field. They walked in rows of twos. Ben was way up ahead of Craig as they made their way through the corridors.

Once they got outside, Ms. Page instructed the bears that they had 15 minutes to play. The line separated as some of the bears ran over to the playground and others headed over to the field to join another class in a game of kick ball that had already gotten started.

Craig saw Ben heading over to the jungle gym where a small group of bears had already gathered. He rushed to catch up with him.

Craig introduces himself. Ben is a little bit taller than Craig. He seems very nice. Ben tells Craig that his family moved to Crownsville during the summer. Ben lives on the other side of town. He has an older brother who is 9 years old. The two quickly become friends. Recess is over before they know it. Ms. Page asks the boys to line up at the door. Craig and Ben agree to try to meet again at lunchtime.

Craig and Ben sit next to each other at the lunch table. Craig has been storing up some questions that he wants to ask Ben. He does not know quite how to go about getting started and then decides to just jump right in. Craig asks Ben why he thinks that he and Ben look so different from the rest of the bears in the class.

Ben tells Craig that his parents told him that he is originally from another city not too far away from Crownsville where many other solid colored bears live. Ben tells Craig that in this city there are other solid colored bears who are either blue, green, or even pink or violet. Ben then tells Craig that his parents told him that he was adopted. Being adopted, Ben continues, means that his parents picked him especially to come to live with their family. Craig finds out that Ben has a second set of parents who live in the other city. Ben has actually met them once! Ben's mother and father took Ben on a trip to that city when he was just a small bear. Ben also tells Craig that he sometimes speaks to his other parents on the telephone.

Craig listens closely to everything that Ben has to tell him. His heart starts pounding like crazy in his chest and he feels himself getting nervous and scared again. He wonders what all of this means for him!

During library hour later on that very same day, Craig decides to ask the librarian to help him find a book about solid colored bears. The librarian is a tall, stern-looking bear lady who whispers and points Craig toward a corner near the windows. Craig sees three different books about solid colored bears. He chooses one that has a big green bear on the cover! Craig checks out the book to take home.

That night, Craig can't wait until bedtime! He has decided that for now he wants to keep the book a secret. That night after lights out he reads under the covers with his flashlight until late into the night.

He finds out that everything Ben has told him is true! There is a city not too far away where lots of solid colored bears live! At that moment, Craig decides that he has to travel to that city to see if he, too, has another set of parents there just like Ben. Tomorrow he will ask Ben if Ben would like to join him on a trip to that city.

During the days to come, the two hash out a plan to travel together secretly to the other city. The book that Craig had taken out from the library includes a little map. The map shows that one has to travel northeast in order to find that city. Craig tells Ben about the map and explains to him that he has a compass that his grandfather gave him on his birthday that will help them make sure that they won't get lost. Ben tells Craig that he has been on the bus a few times with his brother and parents. Ben tells Craig that there is a bus stop close to their school from where buses leave to go in all different directions. The two decide that they will sneak off after school on Friday...

On Friday morning Craig packs some snacks, his cell phone, and his compass in his backpack along with money from his piggy bank. Craig's mom told Craig the night before that she might *be* a few minutes late that day after school to pick him up because she has an appointment for his two little sisters. Ben usually takes the school bus home.

The two manage to make it out of the door quickly at the end of the school day and run as fast as their legs could carry them to the bus stop on the main street of town. So nervous that they may get caught, they arrive at the bus stop out of breath! Craig and Ben plop themselves down on the bench to wait for the bus...

One bus pulls up to the bus stop. When the doors open up the two ask the bus driver if the bus is heading northeast. The bus driver shakes his head no. Then he explains that the northeast bus will be the next one to come along. Indeed, just a few minutes later, another bus pulls into the bus stop. Craig and Ben jump onboard, relieved that they have not gotten caught...

The trip seems to take forever! They run out of games to play and get tired of looking out the windows. Craig is hungry. They had finished all of their snacks quickly into the trip. Ben gets cranky and tired.

After a while they both fall asleep.

Suddenly the bus comes to a complete stop.

Craig and Ben awaken to the face of the big burly bus driver staring down at them. "You boys fell asleep. This is the last stop! Where are you going? Where are your parents? Are you alone? Are you lost?" Craig and Ben rub their eyes and look around... They are the last ones on the bus and it is starting to get dark!

Suddenly Craig and Ben get scared. The bus has pulled into a big bus station. Lots of buses are parked side-by-side. Lots of bears are rushing around, getting onto buses and getting off of buses. Some buses are pulling out of the station, others are coming in. Suddenly they feel very alone and lost. Craig tries to answer the bus driver's questions and his voice comes out all shaky and small. He starts to explain to the bus driver that Ben and he have traveled to the city to try to meet his other parents. Then Craig remembers his cell phone! Just as he is about to unpack it and call his mom the phone rings! It is Craig's mom! She is crying with relief as she hears Craig's voice answering the phone.

She says, "Craig, we have been so worried about you!" She explains to Craig that she wants to speak with the bus driver. Craig hands the phone to the bus driver. After a while the bus driver hands the phone back to Craig. Craig's mom tells Craig that the bus driver is going to take Craig and Ben to a safe place and that they should stay there and wait for her to come to pick them up. After Craig is finished talking to his mom, the bus driver becomes a little friendlier. He takes the boys inside the bus station into an office where there is a secretary who offers Craig and Ben hot chocolate and cookies.

When Craig's mom arrives she is relieved to see the two of them. She is *so* happy that they are safe that she is not angry. She gives both of them a great big hug. She has brought along warm jackets for Craig and Ben for the trip back home.

After delivering Ben safely to his home that night, Craig's parents sit him down in the living room in order to have a heart-to-heart talk with him. They tell Craig the story of how it was the happiest day in their lives when they were able to welcome Craig into their home to come to live with them to be their son. They promise Craig that he can ask all the questions in the world that he wants. They assure him that they will stay up as long as they need to until all of his questions get answered.

DISCUSSION QUESTIONS

Why do you think Craig is so scared when he overhears his parents talking to his grandparents the night of his birthday party?

What are some of the thoughts going through Craig's mind when he tosses and turns in bed that night?

What is Craig feeling and thinking when he first sees Ben?

Why does Craig keep the book about solid colored bears a secret from his parents and sisters?

What does Craig expect to find when he travels to the city with Ben?

What do you think might be some questions Craig may ask his parents at the end of the book?

Below are a few of the questions that Craig might have for his parents:

- What does it mean to be adopted?

- Why are some bears adopted and others are not?

- What happens to the bears that do not get adopted?

- Where did I come from?

- How come my sisters are not adopted?

- Do you love me the same as my sisters?

- Can I get sent back to where I came from?

- Will I always be able to stay with you?

- What do you think Craig's parents will say to Craig during their heart-to-heart talk at the end of the book?

- How will Craig's parents talk to Craig about his having run away with Ben?

- How would Craig's sisters feel and/or treat Craig if they found out that he was adopted?

- Why do you think Craig's parents never told him that he was adopted before?

- Is a 6 year old ready to deal with finding out about being adopted?

- What cautions/strategies should be used to discuss adoption with a 6 year old?

- What if Craig were 8 or 10 years old?

ACKNOWLEDGMENTS

Many thanks to Allen Donahue for his steadfast encouragement and many hours of work, to Samuel Feinberg for his invaluable contributions, edits, suggestions and so much support, to Bert Holtje for his guidance and generosity, to Joan Fiorello whose wisdom and kindness helped to keep me going throughout the project, to Debra Castaldo for her encouragement, to Frank Sileo for helping me stay positive and for sharing his experiences as an author, to Daryl Solomon for nurturing my creative process, to Margaret Blackler for her guidance and support, to the sales representative in the children's book department at the Barnes & Noble store at Riverside Square mall in Hackensack, New Jersey, to Rita and Ezra, the two children I met at Barnes & Noble who cheered me on in February of 2008 and to Kaitlyn Berg, to all of my patients, and to my family and friends for all of their love and support.

ABOUT THE ILLUSTRATOR

Allen E. Donahue is a self-taught graphic artist who is originally from Willingboro, New Jersey. Mr. Donahue graduated from JFK High School. Currently he does free-lance work from his home in Ventnor City, New Jersey.

ABOUT THE AUTHOR
OF THE DISCUSSION SECTION

Samuel Feinberg (Ph.D., NYU) is a licensed psychologist and certified school psychologist who is currently a Clinical Professor of Psychology at Fairleigh Dickinson University, where he coordinates internships and externships and supervises cases at the Psychological Services Clinic. He was previously a practicing and supervising school psychologist for over four decades. Dr. Feinberg has provided extensive counseling and support services to many adopted children and their families. He lives in New York City with his wife Doris and his two grown children, Jennifer and Joshua.

THE END